Coach Gs Formula to Dream, Believe and Achieve

ACHIEVING SUCCESS

A PLAYBOOK MANUAL TO THE GAME OF LIFE

SHANAE B. GOVAN

Printed in the USA by A2Z Books, LLC. Copyright by Shanae B Govan. All rights reserved. This book or any portion thereof may not be reproduced or used in any manner whatsoever without the express written permission of the publisher except for the use of brief quotations in book review Printed in the United States. First Printing ISBN 978-1-943284-51-1 www.A2ZBookspublishing.net

This Planner Belongs To

_____

_____

> ❝
> *If you want to enjoy and be happy in life, you have to in some ways say goodbye to your former self.*
>
> Steve Nash

Commited Letter *To Self*

  Today, I vow to take the necessary steps towards a successful life. I will choose to put each procedure provided into action by completing the proper moves in order to achieve the goals that I will set for my future. I will not allow the fear of failing to haunt me. Today, I am dedicating my time to pursuing my future. I will not look back or dwell on my past. I am moving forward in a positive direction without ceasing. Today is a new day, and I am going to come after everything that has my name attached to it.

Sincerely,

Your Name:

_____

STEP ONE
Acknowledge the *Winner in You*

You cannot go into the game with a losing mentality. Your thoughts must shift to believing that you are a winner! Often, we allow previous obstacles that have invaded our lives to somehow destroy our confidence. In this cycle of success, there is no room for that kind of behavior. We must think like an overcomer. We should talk and walk like we've already won the victory! People ought to see triumph through the way we carry ourselves. Our ambiance should mirror success. Internally, you may be feeling that you are on your last leg, but no one should ever know it! Your current circumstance doesn't determine your final destination.

It is important to not allow where you are now to predict your future. Many times, our "now moments" cause mental roadblocks that steer us from our destiny. Champions do not always win every fight; they learn to endure the road towards adversity which puts them in the position to be a winner. Our value isn't found in what we have materialistically or what we do not have. You're rich when you have strong will power and determination to push yourself beyond setbacks and detours. Your thought process and the ability to evaluate and breakdown situations in an effective way allow you to be a champion.

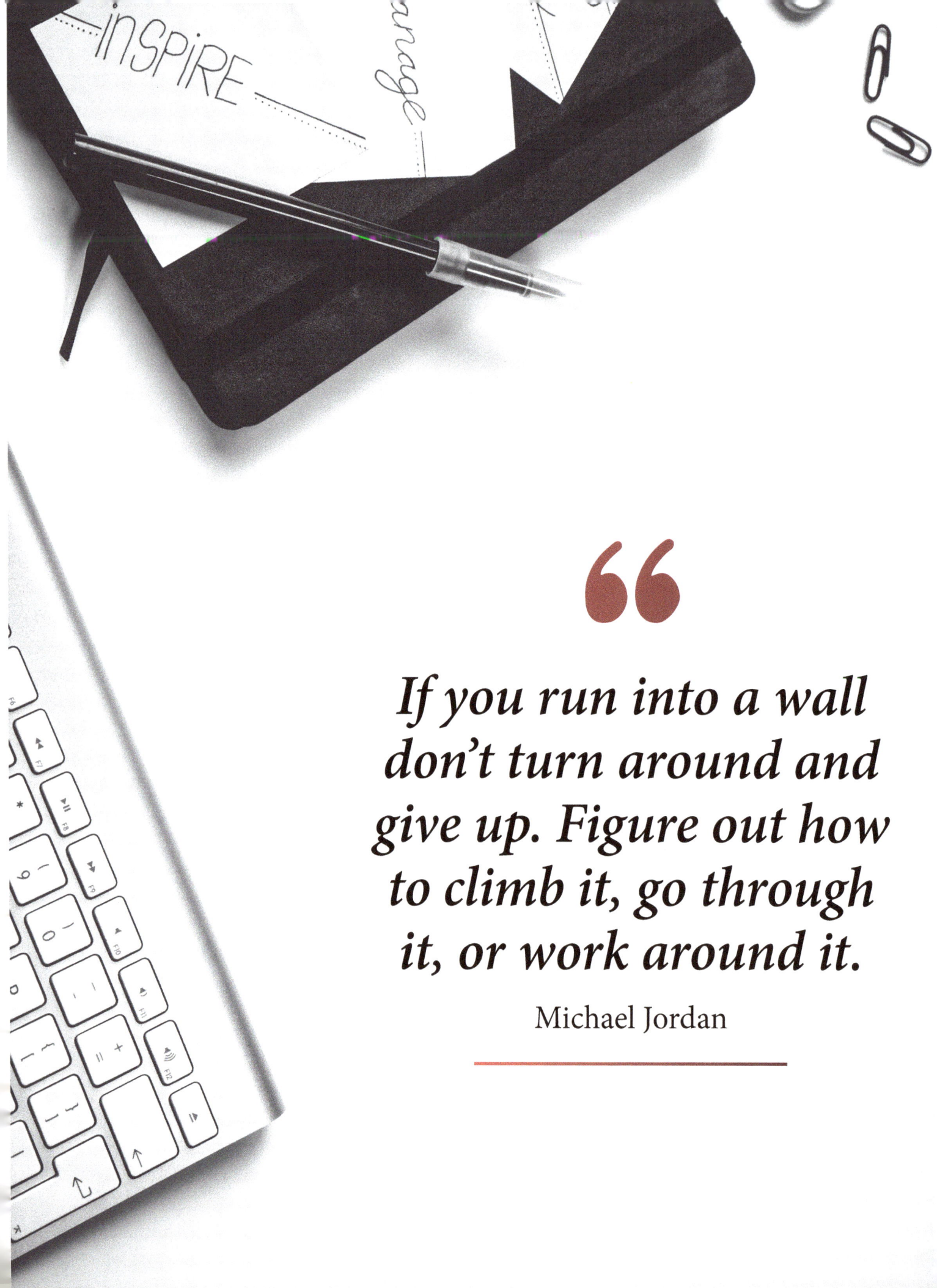

> *If you run into a wall don't turn around and give up. Figure out how to climb it, go through it, or work around it.*
>
> Michael Jordan

The "Successful way of thinking Step-Up Process" has a chain reaction that effects the way we perceive ourselves.

"If you can think it, then it becomes a part of your vocabulary. Next, it will become carried out in your actions".

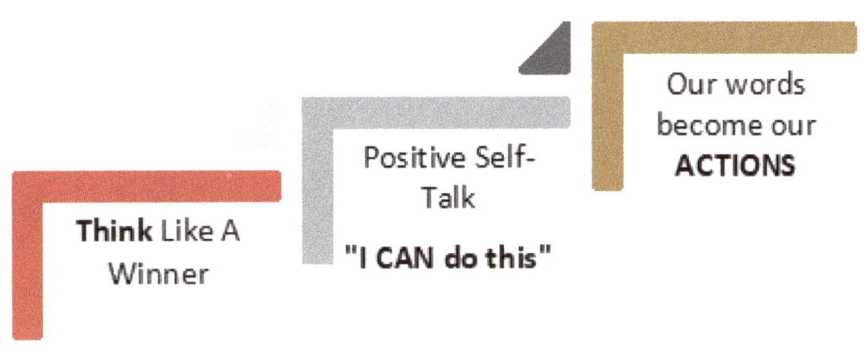

Below is a chart that gives examples of words that define a winner's mentality. List FIVE positive words that describe the winner in you!

LIST FIVE POSITIVE WORDS THAT DEFINE THE WINNER WITHIN YOU; EXAMPLES	
	OVERCOMER
	HARD WORKING
	DRIVEN
	DETERMINED
	DEDICATED

1. _____
2. _____
3. _____
4. _____
5. _____

NOTES

STEP TWO
Understand that defeat is a *part of the Journey*

Nothing comes easy to someone with greatness attached to their lives! Our failures make us stronger. Low and isolated positions have a way of birthing another level of maturity in us. Many times we become stuck in between a rock and a hard place for several reasons. The first is because no one rejoices over being mentally defeated. We have encompassed this fairytale way of thinking that has us living in a false reality; which in result doesn't prepare us when hard times show up! We're too busy watching the Beyoncé's and Jay Z's while admiring their successes, but we forget that there was a cost to their glamorous lifestyle; it's called "Adversity".

Failing at something is laced with purpose. I don't know anyone who has started a business who did not at first, run into difficulty getting it off the ground. I'm sure they had phases of financial challenges. Those are expected. It teaches you the gift of pushing beyond the defeated place. Those things allow us to appreciate every stage of development and growth. Each period gets you prepared for the big stage. Often, we tap out too soon and forfeit our rights to the top! Don't tap out before its time.

Defeated moments should not push you to a dark place in your mind. Live beyond those circumstances mentally. If you want to write a book, do not look at the fact that you do not have the finances to cover the expenses; write it first, and then allow each step to take care of itself afterwards. Several of us lose out before the race begins because of the way we perceive ourselves. Value up! Believe that you can do anything that you put your mind to.

Failure does not come from losing, but from not trying.

Larry Brown

List 3 experiences you have had where you failed at something and explain below how it made you feel.

Being defeated is often a temporary condition. Giving up is what makes it permanent.

Marilyn Vos Savant

1. Describe how you feel.
___
___

Did you try again?   Yes ☐   No ☐
If No, why not?
___
___

2. Describe how you feel.
___
___

Did you try again?   Yes ☐   No ☐
If No, why not?
___
___

3. Describe how you feel.
___
___

Did you try again?   Yes ☐   No ☐
If No, why not?
___
___

NOTES

STEP THREE
Prepare for the *Destination*

We are hardly ever held responsible for the things that bombard our lives unexpectedly. When you know in your heart that you have goals and ambitions, although your future is unborn, why not prepare early for where you are headed; therefore, when you make your arrival you won't have to spend time trying to adjust to the position because your preparation has set you up to be ahead of the game.

Don't get me wrong; it's good to wait in patience and expectancy. But the difference in that and wasting time are totally different. Opportunities of success come once in a lifetime. Just consider how much time we would waste if we sat around waiting on things to happen, instead of preparing for them now. We cannot control our past or our future, but we are responsible for our present. Studying for an exam today will benefit me for tomorrow. My preparation will determine my outcome.

Michael Jordan didn't wait to get ready for his upcoming opponents the day before the game; He prepared before time. Your preparation should mirror where you are on your way to. People should see you and discover the fragrance of where you're trying to go. Millionaires were not born overnight, unless you inherited it at birth. Most successful business people, have a story of how they prepared for where they currently are. Preparing for the destination you must divorce yourself from the opinions of others. Sometimes our preparation will make many people uncomfortable, especially if they're intimidated by your ability to get ahead. That comes with the territory.

> *Don't spend so much time trying to choose the perfect opportunity, that you miss the right opportunity*
>
> Michael Dell

Below is a "Preparation Chart"

List the necessary components asked of you in the boxes

_____
_____
_____

_____
_____
_____

Prepare
List ways you've prepared for your future.

Plan
List plans you've put in place to obtain your goal.

Practice
List ways you've put your plan into practice.

Produce
List examples of how you have produced results from your practice.

_____
_____
_____

_____
_____
_____

NOTES

STEP FOUR
Make Drop-Offs *when Necessary*

Anything that's carrying too much baggage must go through a drop-off phase to lighten the load for the ride ahead! We must know who is riding in our ship. Anything or anyone that is not helping the advancement of the journey does not deserve to be on board. This element of processing is one of the most difficult for people to do; naturally we all carry more things than we should which prohibits our transition towards our set goals.

It is very important that to reach success you know when it's time to walk away from things and people. I have experienced first-hand what it is like to forfeit rights to destiny because of having the wrong people in my circle. During this stage of development, you cannot be afraid to abandon anything that doesn't help you become successful. This doesn't mean you have to use people to get where you desire to be, it just means that you're mature enough to know who deserves to be around you and who is not.

Don't mistake seasonal people for individuals who are connected to your destiny. This really is one of the toughest components that we as human beings struggle with because we are afraid to hurt those who we've become familiar with having around. Let's not confuse being comfortable with growing with the right people. Let's just be honest; everyone doesn't have intentions on seeing you win. It becomes necessary to deplete these people from your circle in order to advance further.

Delayed journeys are usually a result of being among the wrong people. You must surround yourself with likeminded individuals and also winners; people who will push you. We don't benefit from not being in acquaintance with people who do not see us beyond where we currently are. My circle is small, but carries a lot of weight. I have mentors, advocates, and other believers who I am connected to. They correct me when I'm wrong, but also cover me with grace when necessary. Those are the kinds of people we must remain connected to if we want to obtain success.

In the table below list the TOP 5 people in your circle and explain what they add/subtract to or from your life. This is a tool to help prioritize who is necessary to keep on board, and who may need to be removed from your circle in order to keep your life moving in the right direction. Associations and who you allow to be in connection to you are very important!

Name: _____

Assets or Liability?

_____

Contributions?

_____

Name: _____

Assets or Liability?

_____

Contributions?

_____

Name: _____

Assets or Liability?

_____

Contributions?

_____

Name: _____

Assets or Liability?

_____

Contributions?

_____

Name: _____

Assets or Liability?

_____

Contributions?

_____

NOTES

STEP FIVE
Value what you bring *to the table*

Value Up! It's very essential that you understand that no one will appreciate your gift and honor it the way you can. Do not seek for validation through words of affirmation. Although those words can pump us up, what good do they hold if you don't value what you offer beforehand? It serves us nothing to downplay ourselves or lower who we are to make others feel comfortable. If you're good at baking, start a bake sell. Just because Mrs. Susie likes to make pies, doesn't mean that you can't do the same, especially if you're good at it. Invest in your gift.

If God blessed you with a beautiful voice, and someone compliments you, don't reply by saying "I hate my voice, or I really can't sing". That's negative self-talk. You can be humble and accept a compliment. All of those things have everything to do with you having the ability to value what you bring to the table. We all do it. But it is something that we must abandon if we desire to succeed in life.

> # *When you start seeing your worth, you'll find it harder to stay around people who don't.*
>
> Unknown

Below list 3 talents that you have and the qualities that make you good at them! Be creative and think outside the box! Do not limit yourself!

Name of talent: _____

Qualities:

_____
_____
_____
_____

Name of talent: _____

Qualities:

_____
_____
_____
_____

Name of talent: _____

Qualities:

_____
_____
_____
_____

NOTES

STEP SIX
Be willing to Change *in order to grow*

Growth requires change. Because growing is probably one of the most difficult things to do, we often find ourselves stagnate. There are two forms of growth; the first is forced change. This constitutes that something has occurred in your life which has pushed you to a place where this was the only available option! The second type comes by making a choice.

Situations occur in our lives that give us no other choice besides to change how we think, the way we do things or even who we interact with. Those driving forces in our lives help us; although in the moment of being pushed to adjust may not feel the best, it is always what we need in order to continue on the path towards our goals.

Being committed in making sound decisions is always a place that we desire to be in within our lives. Once you experience how powerful it is to make "decisions" that will lead you down a healthy pathway, then decision making becomes easier especially when the results attached are always positive! With both forms of growth, they both are connected to having faith in what you're committing to.

So, if you never take a leap of faith to jump and venture out on possibilities then you will stunt your growth. Don't allow fear to grip your heart. Power up and do the grown-up thing; it's called "The Power of a Decision"! I made one choice that led to the greatest blessing of my life. I decided to write, which the end result caused me to become an entrepreneur! That is literally all it takes. I knew that one day I wanted to have a business, so I had to make the decision to do what it took to seal that in order to grow! Just Jump as Steve Harvey suggested!

> *Never say never, because Limits like Fears, are often just an illusion*
>
> — *Michael Jordan*

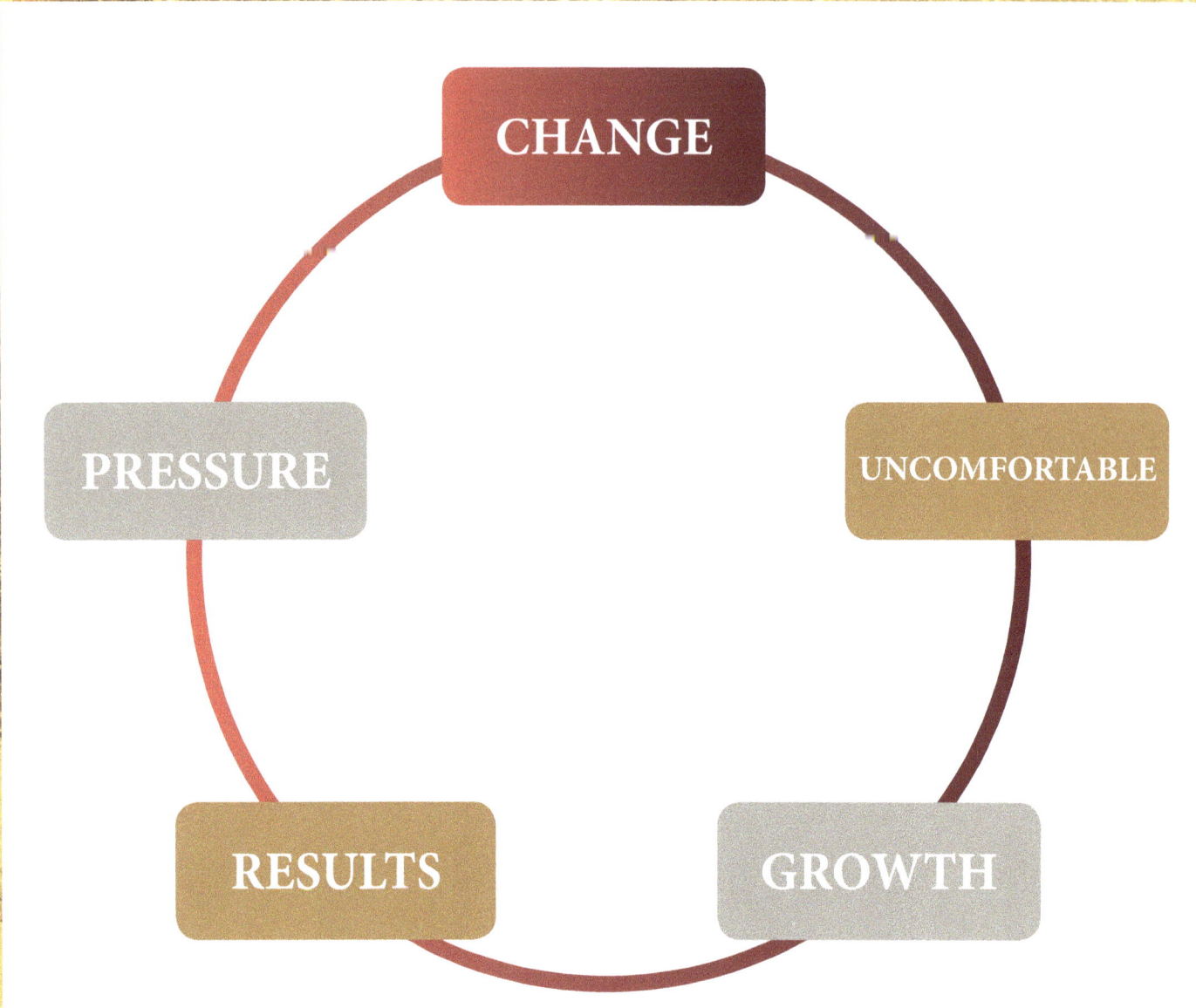

Above is a cycle chart that describes the cycle of change. It will produce what we need in order to gain the results necessary to obtain our goal!! Commit to the shift!!

NOTES

STEP SEVEN
Learn to *Trust Others*

I believe that everyone deserves the opportunity to be trusted until it is compromised. Too many times we miss out on our blessings from operating in our old habits that has taught us "Trust no one". Who really can advance in life with that way of thinking? How will you have business partners or successful relationships without trust? It is one of the most essential tools that allow relationships to flourish. I understand things happen that make us put up walls unintentionally but it should never be to the point where we knock ourselves out of the race towards destiny! Learning to trust is an art! We all must develop this responsibility if we want to win in life!

The first component to learning to trust others comes with the acceptance of understanding that you may get let down. That's a part of it. No one is perfect. Trust lays the foundation of successful and meaningful relationships. It also brings awareness of what each individual mean to the partnership. It is impossible to thrive in this life without the ability to trust and coincide with other individuals. I mean who honestly wants to live a life with the thought of not being able or wanting to have a belief system in others. It detours us from getting to our destination. Trust is an essential tool that is necessary and we must all acquire this trait if we want to win in life!

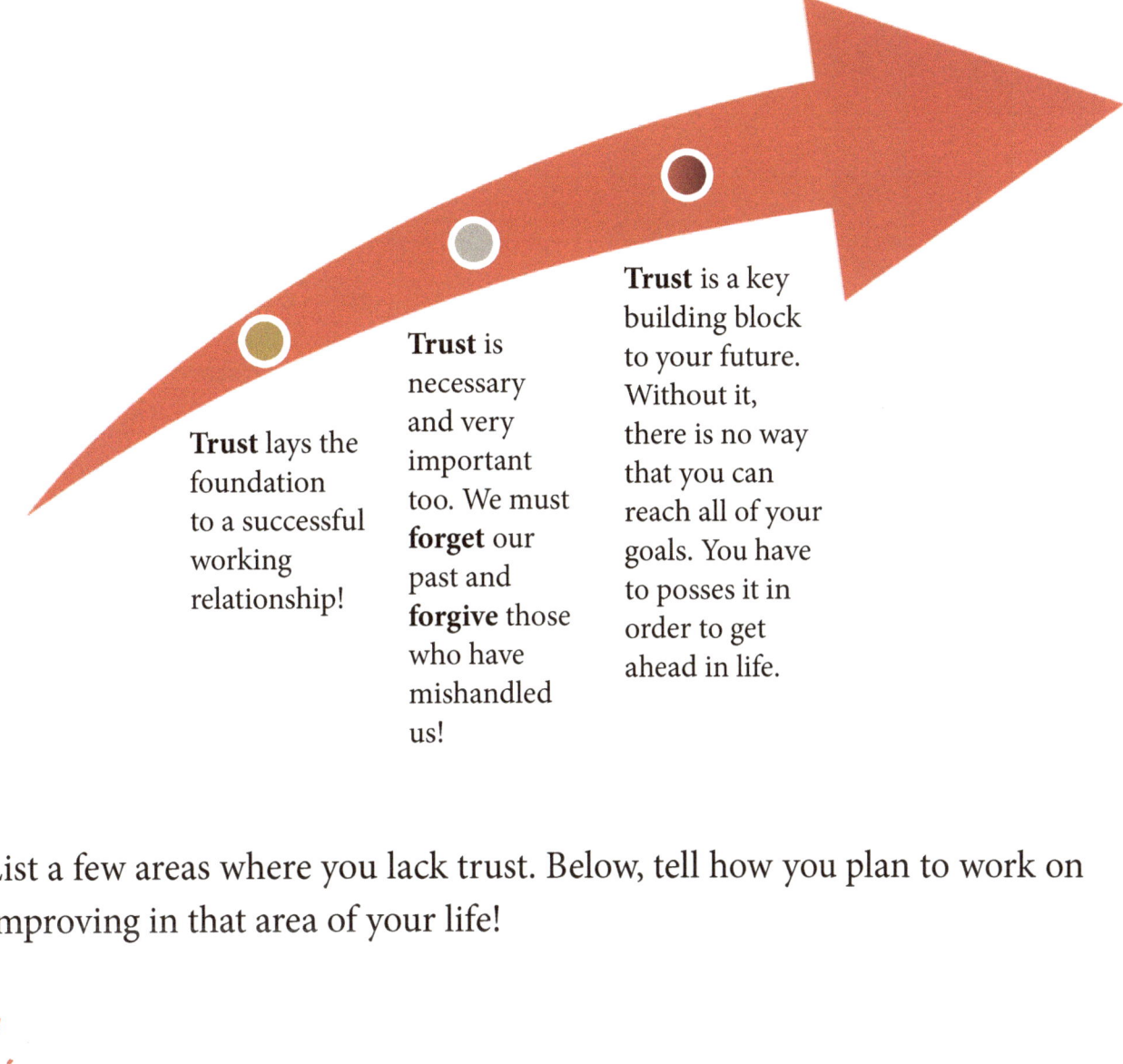

Trust lays the foundation to a successful working relationship!

Trust is necessary and very important too. We must **forget** our past and **forgive** those who have mishandled us!

Trust is a key building block to your future. Without it, there is no way that you can reach all of your goals. You have to posses it in order to get ahead in life.

List a few areas where you lack trust. Below, tell how you plan to work on improving in that area of your life!

1. _____

2. _____

3. _____

NOTES

STEP EIGHT

Don't waste time on *Unnecessary Things*

Often, we find ourselves giving too much energy to things that do not matter. We worry ourselves about elements that serve no purpose and lead us down a path that lends us a broken harvest. I have acquired the desire to shift my focus only on things worth my attention. Feed your focus with positive things. Hopefully these things will be geared toward your future; nothing that will prohibit you from prospering. If someone wronged you, let it go! Do not waste time on things that serve no purpose or benefit towards helping get to your destiny.

Your focus should be so engulfed with becoming a better you daily that whatever happened in the past is a non-factor. True winners keep their eyes on the prize! Success is a journey that all of us have the opportunity to attain but your willingness and ability to remain focused on the necessary components of life will determine your outcome. Stay Hungry! What's fueling your focus?

> *Don't waste your time looking back for what you have lost; MOVE ON for life was not meant to be traveled backwards*

— Unknown

List 3 things that you need to let go of in order to move forward with your life!!!!

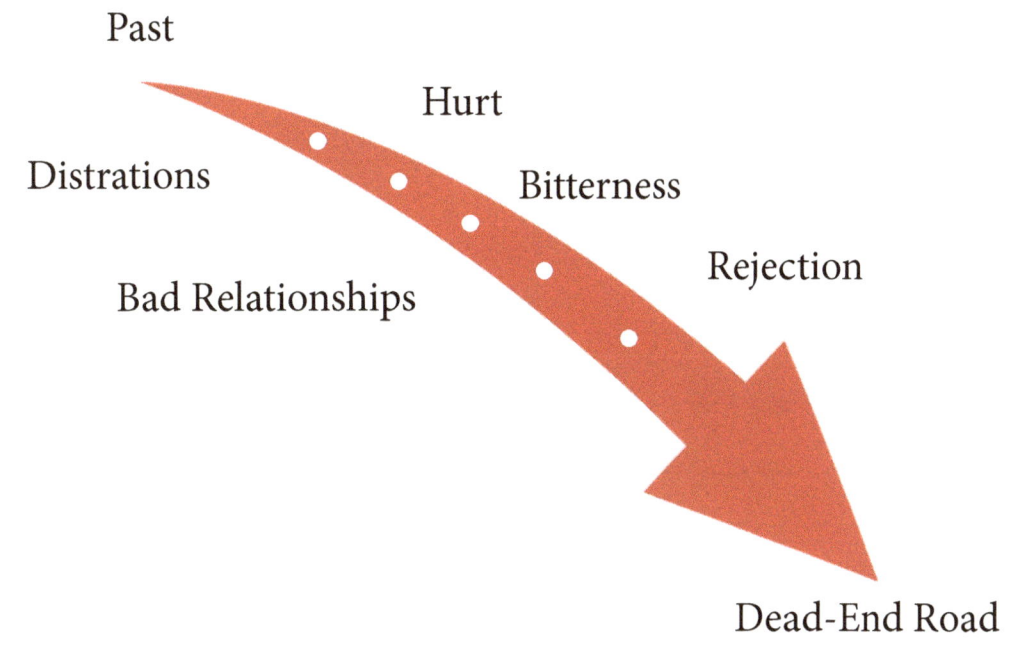

1. _____

2. _____

3. _____

NOTES

STEP NINE
Believe in *Your Grind*

Don't become so distracted by what others have going on in their lives that you forget what investments and deposits you're making. What you're working towards is important and of great significance also. It may not look like anyone else's grind but it is valued because it belongs to you! Often I hear so many people comparing their chapter 8 with someone else's chapter 48 and they forget that there are levels to each of our stories. Posture yourself to value what you are doing and what steps you're making to get there. If someone on the next block bought a new car and you're driving your parent's vehicle that's okay. Keep working on your credit so you can get your dream house, car, boat, or whatever it is that you desire to have. This is the right way to go about things instead of trying to keep up with your neighbors! Trust your investments and do not allow time or anyone rush your growth process! We only push ourselves out of the race when we try to live according to someone else's journey. Believe in your grind and stick to it! Step by step, trust it and do not waiver from what you have set out to achieve!

Below is a flow chart modeling the reflected process of your preparation!! Follow the suggested points below

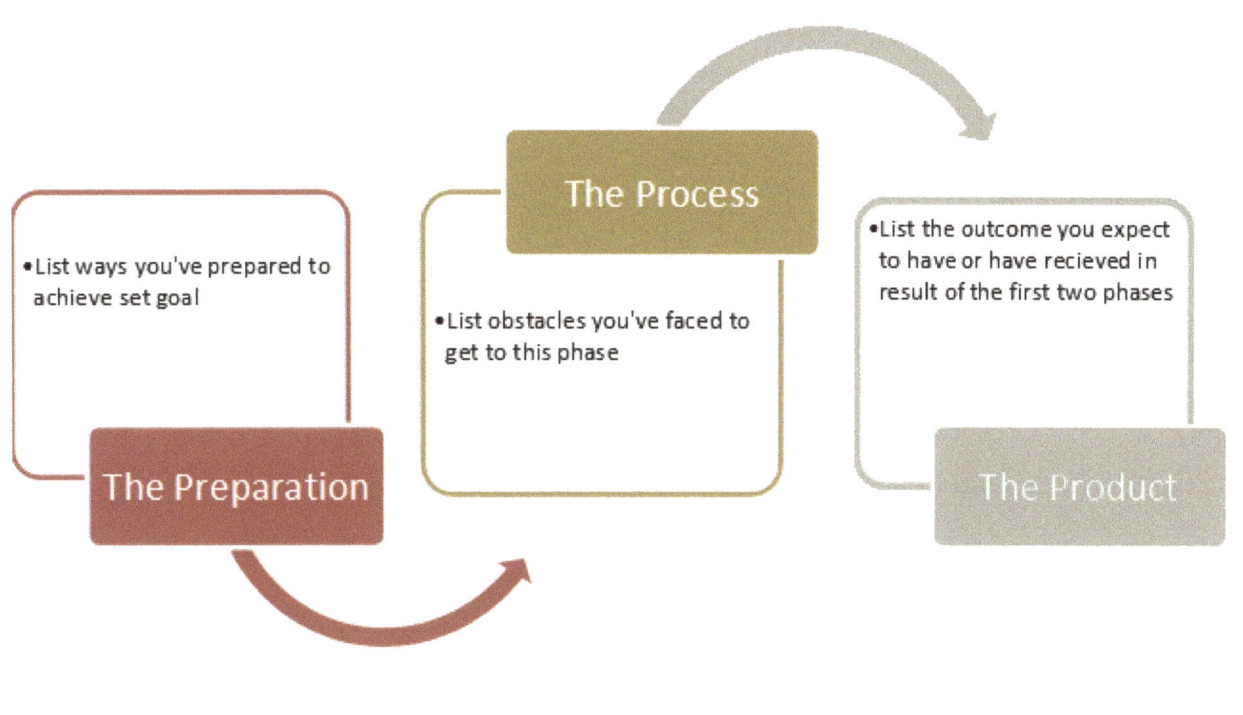

NOTES

STEP TEN
Connect with *Successful People*

My circle is small. Of my few friends most of them are probably doing better than I am. This allows me to grow. I have a mentor who is a certified life coach which is the next thing on my plate that I plan to accomplish. Others, who I am connected to, are college coaches, people with successful businesses, marriages, careers. Currently, I am a head high school basketball coach, but one of my goals within the next five years is to accomplish becoming a head college basketball coach. I stay close to people who are in high rank because it challenges me; I never become complacent or wish to settle. Many of us are intimidated by people who are doing better than we are so to remain comfortable we remain stuck around individuals who are either of equal ranking in success as we are or among those who have little to nothing going on. We don't realize that this is stunting our growth! How can they tell you the way to get to the next level if they've never been there? We all have to check our circle from time to time. That doesn't mean walk around thinking you're better than others, it just means be mindful of who's pouring into your future. Chickens and Eagles cannot hangout; one can fly and the other doesn't have that ability. Connect to likeminded people who will help push you to be better and open the door for you to achieve success!!

> **The strength of the team is each individual member.**
>
> *The strength of each member is the team*
>
> — Phil Jackson

In the chart below, list 3 goals that you have. Reflect on how your circle contributes or takes away from you achieving what you've put on your goal sheet. Remember, we can only go as far as the people we are connected to. Your circle is a reflection of who you are!

30 / 60 / 90

Goal 1

_____

_____

Goal 2

_____

_____

Goal 3

_____

_____

NOTES

STEP ELEVEN
Don't be afraid to Jump

Steve Harvey wrote an awarding winning best-selling book encouraging readers to Jump! Take the leap of faith and do it without any regards! Commit to whatever goal you set and go after it with all you have! Jump! It is so easy to find ourselves going around the same mountain out of the fear of failing. Nothing prosperous can result from remaining in a comfort zone; allow the uncomfortable place to push you into your NEXT! Leap out on faith and trust what you are expecting to obtain! When I wrote my first book, I had no idea about how to publish, moreover how to write. But I stepped out and went for it. And as I write now, I am in the process of publishing my third one in less than three years! It's all about doing the hard part first. Jumping is easy but the difficulty comes with the preparation! Have you prepared to Jump?

> **Success is never final;
> Failure is never fatal.**
> *It is the courage that counts*
>
> John Wooden

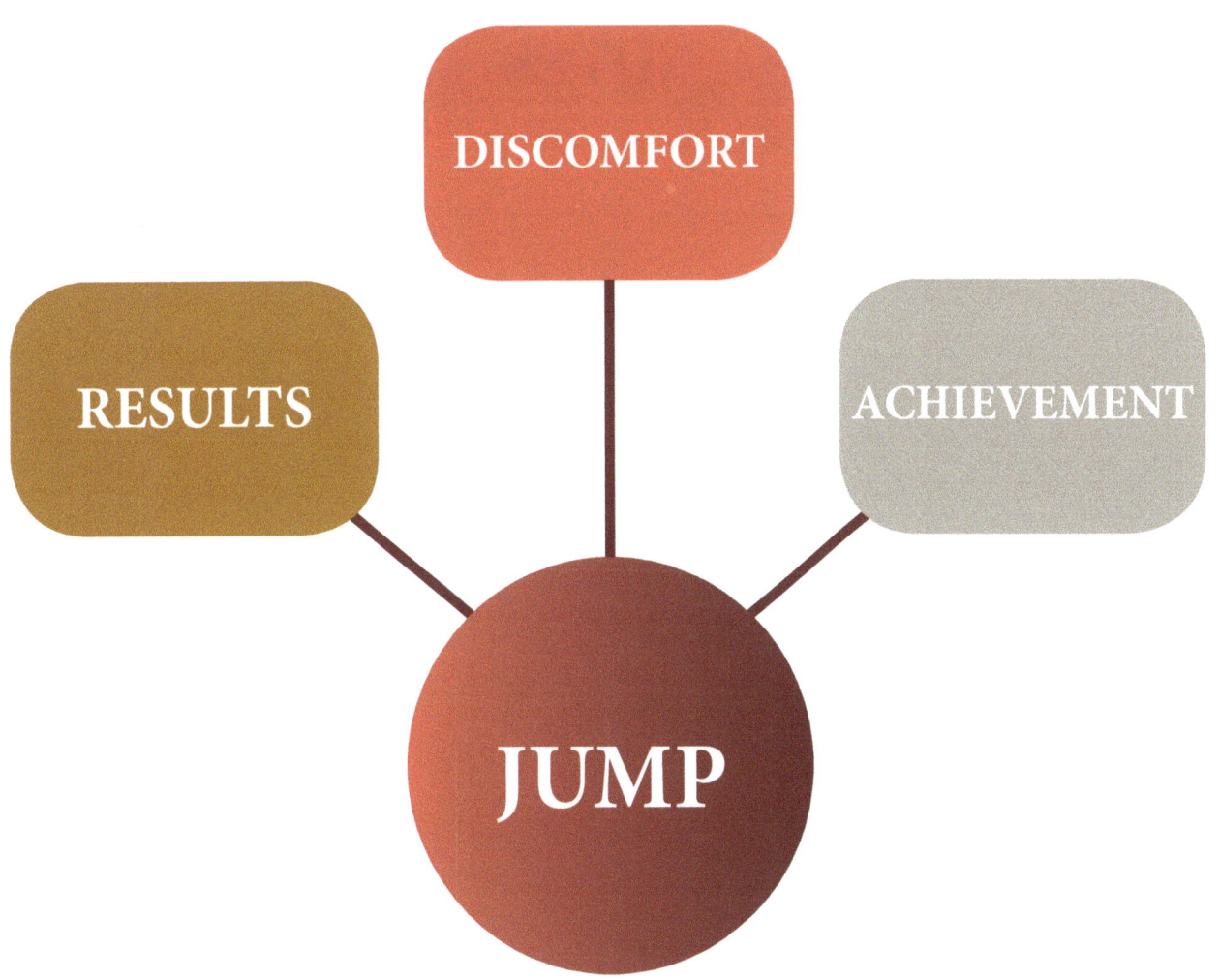

RESULTS:
When you push yourself beyond the limit, you will see results! That's your Reward!

DISCOMFORT:
"It won't always feel good! Sometimes you will want to give up; But you can't afford to!

ACHIEVEMENT:
You will achieve goals that you have set for yourself! Lead by example!

NOTES

STEP TWELVE
Dare To Be Different

One of my strongest qualities that I have had since I was a teenager was the mindset to be different. For many this is often difficult because it's safe to say that we all feel comfortable when we're doing "the norm". Most don't like brining attention to themselves, so instead of standing out, they settle to fit in. Of course being organic will cause you to stand out but that's a key to success; it's impossible to try to fit in with the crowd and be successful. Because you often have to take the road less traveled in order to create your own path and to get different results. Sure there are some blueprints left that we should follow but not to the extent where we walk in the shadow of someone else. Kobe Bryant studied Michael Jordan but he had his own twist on his game. He had to set a new trend to get the results suitable to his trail and mark in history. Each of us has our own path and birth right to our destiny! Walk in your way and own your journey! Do not be afraid to grind so hard that it makes those around you uncomfortable. That's a good thing. Your ambition should be so contagious that it forces those in your circle to either level up or move around!

> **"**
>
> *Everything negative- pressure, challenges, are all an opportunity for me to rise*
>
> Kobe Bryant

Below is a chart the demonstrates the positive effects of being Different

List the Pros of being a Leader and daring to be different!

1 _____

2 _____

3 _____

4 _____

NOTES

STEP THIRTEEN
Graduate from the *Opinion of Others*

We all are assigned critics in life. People are going to give their opinion whether it is wanted or not. That's not important. The most relevant thing is that when running this race in life is that we do not allow what people say to control or dictate our actions! Everyone will not agree with the decisions we make. That goes for family as well. Those things are going to happen. We must remember to give an account to our own choices. Do not give people the power in pushing us to a place to make decisions that they will not be responsible for dealing with the consequences. For every choice made will follow a harvest. Once you grow to the place where you totally commit to yourself rather than how others feel about what you do affect your future, things of that nature will become less and less relevant. It took me a while to grow to this place; honestly I have to remind myself daily that what others think really doesn't matter as long as I'm happy with my choices. Too many times do we commit to caring entirely too much about what people say. Divorce yourself from their opinions and move forward with your life!

> **If you accept the expectations of others especially negative ones, *then you never will change the outcome***
>
> Unknown

Below is a chart showing the relationship of our connections, choices and commitments which should be our driving force to graduate from the opinions of others. List choices you've made and how they reflected who you are connected to and your commitment to those things!

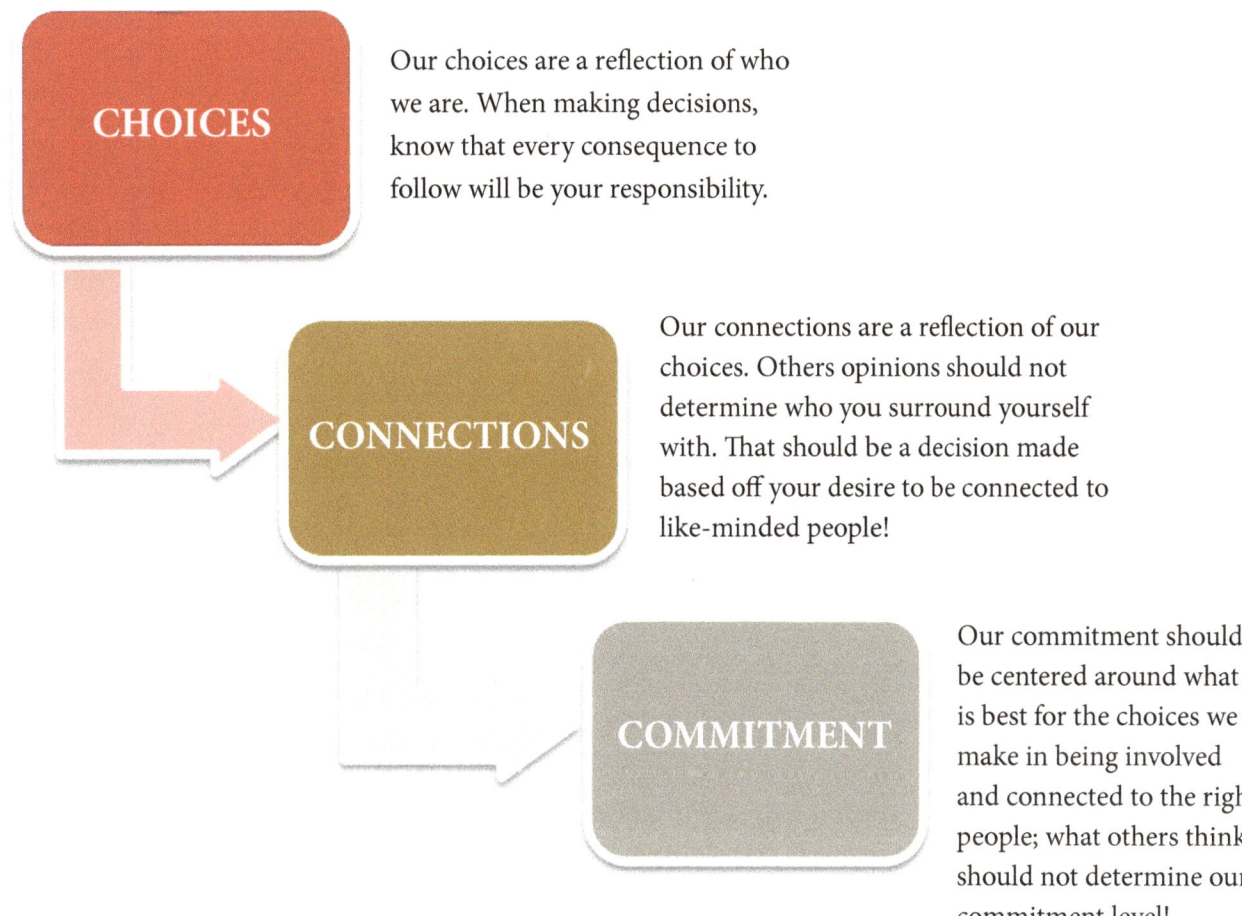

CHOICES — Our choices are a reflection of who we are. When making decisions, know that every consequence to follow will be your responsibility.

CONNECTIONS — Our connections are a reflection of our choices. Others opinions should not determine who you surround yourself with. That should be a decision made based off your desire to be connected to like-minded people!

COMMITMENT — Our commitment should be centered around what is best for the choices we make in being involved and connected to the right people; what others think should not determine our commitment level!

NOTES

STEP FOURTEEN
Celebrate Others

It is important to celebrate the successes of others. This is a necessary trait to carry because you want people to support you when you're doing well. I believe that when we congratulate the achievements of our peers it says a lot about our character. That symbolizes growth and shows that you are not self-centered. We all should have the natural desire to see everyone win. I think we can all attest to having hardships and struggles, so when someone gets ahead or accomplishes a milestone in whatever area of their life, that's something that we should be proud of. In actuality, these things are what help keep us on our feet and motivated. Often, we look at it from the wrong standpoint, not realizing what sacrifices those people have made in order to achieve their goals. For me, growing up in a broken home was enough to keep me focused and striving to have a successful life. I don't think that I should be penalized for my ambition, rather celebrated by those who are genuinely happy for what's taking place. If we would all take on this mindset, life would be so much better! I want everyone to WIN!

> **To build a strong team, you must see someone else's strength as a compliment to your weakness *not a threat to your position or authority***
>
> — Christine Kane

Below is a chart that asks you to list the effects of the two types of people that are listed. Check which one you are. On both sides, tell some characteristics of each of the two.

☐ *Positive Uplifting People* ☐ *Negative Downing People*

_____   _____
_____   _____
_____   _____
_____   _____
_____   _____
_____   _____
_____   _____

NOTES

STEP FIFTEEN
Develop the habit *to grind Daily*

Everyone is given 24 hours out of each day to put forth whatever it is that they may decide to do in that time slot. Some use theirs to be productive, and others choose to waste time either making excuses or simply doing nothing. In order to get a different result, we must do something different. Success is not handed to you. Each opportunity that you are presented, you must take advantage of it. We should push ourselves to develop the appetite to grind on a daily basis. It does not matter what your production consists of as long as it is towards something that will help you achieve whatever you desire to have. Often times we miss opportunities because we waste time in unnecessary areas of our lives. The time that we have to be productive is very important to the keys of our success journey. It should become a habit to have the desire to get something positive done out of your day. You must first have a plan set in place along with steps to accomplish each task.

> *Success is a peace of mind, which is a direct result of self-satisfaction in knowing you made the best effort* to become the best in which you are capable

John Wooden

Tentative 24 Hour Schedule

Below, is listed each hour of the day and the things that you usually are doing at that specific time.

This is a strategy to see if you're using your time wisely or wasting it!

12:00 a.m.	
1:00 a.m.	
2:00 a.m.	
3:00 a.m	
4:00 a.m.	
5:00 a.m.	
6:00 a.m.	
7:00 a.m.	
8:00 a.m.	
9:00 a.m	
10:00 a.m.	
11:00 a.m.	
12:00 p.m.	
1:00 p.m.	
2:00 p.m	
3:00 p.m.	
4:00 p.m.	
5:00 p.m	
6:00 p.m.	
7:00 p.m.	
8:00 p.m.	
9:00 p.m.	
10:00 p.m.	
11:00 p.m.	
12:00 a.m.	

Are you spending most of your day being productive or unproductive? Explain below how you will change your habits and behaviors to become more productive if you are not doing so.

_____

_____

_____

_____

_____

_____

_____

_____

_____

_____

_____

_____

_____

Interested in Writing and/or Publishing a book? Visit www.A2ZBookspublishing.net

www.ingramcontent.com/pod-product-compliance
Lightning Source LLC
Chambersburg PA
CBHW051349110526
44591CB00025B/2954